Pneumatrix

Expressed by Derly Andre

Illustrated by Heidi Guedel

Edited and Foreword by Arnold G. Tijerina, III

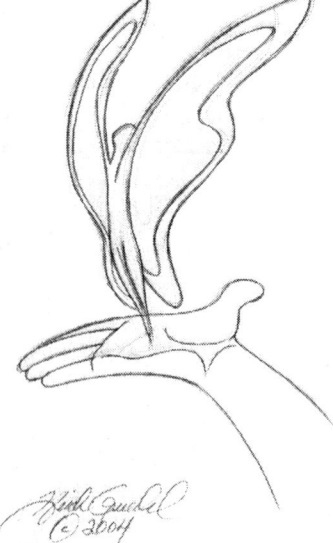

For information, contact

TICO Publishing, 25045 Jaclyn Avenue, Moreno Valley, CA 92557
(951) 452-2277

First Printing 2005

Andre, Derly

      Pneumatrix: A Poetic Soul / Tico Publishing
      ISBN 1-59457-729-3 (hardcover)
      1.   Books---United States---Poetry.
      I.   Andre, Derly, 1956-
      II.   II. Title.

Library of Congress Control Number: 2004110844
Publisher: BookSurge, LLC
North Charleston, South Carolina

ATTENTION: WRITING & PUBLISHING ORGANIZATIONS, PREMIUM INCENTIVE BUYERS, EDUCATIONAL INSTITUTIONS, AND INDUSTRY PUBLICATIONS:

Quantity discounts are available on bulk purchases of this book for reselling, educational purposes, subscription incentives, gifts, or fund raising. Special books or book excerpts can also be created to fit specific needs. For information, please contact our Special Sales Department at Tico Publishing, 25045 Jaclyn Avenue, Moreno Valley, CA 92557. (951) 452-2277.

Interior arrangement/formatting by
kathrine rend
Rend Graphics
www.rendgraphics.com

*Pneumatrix

Expressed by
Derly Andre

Illustrated by
Heidi Guedel

Edited and Foreword by
Arnold G. Tijerina, III

* *pneuma – vital spirit or soul (in ancient Greek pneuma meant both spirit and air)*
* *matrix – a configuration of elements that establishes a relationship for calculation or comparison; an environment from which a thing proceeds or has its origin*

Acknowledgements

Thanks to the many people who have inspired the content of this book through their direct and indirect participation but mostly through their influence on the author.

Thanks to all the local bookstores that still hang in there and take chances on unknown authors.

Thanks to Amazon.com, Barnes & Noble, Borders, and all the other venues though which this book will become available to the masses.

Thanks to the City of Austin, Texas for providing a great home and community for the author for the last 18 years.

And last, but most important, thanks to the reader who saw this book, purchased it, was inspired by it and told a friend about it.

Foreword

When I was first contacted in regards to Pneumatrix, I had my doubts as to the marketability of the book. Frankly, the poetry genre is not filled with national bestsellers with the exception of dead poets, for the most part. Seeing as a member of the "Dead Poets Society" did not submit this book to me, I was skeptical.

Becoming a living, bestselling poet is similar to getting into the National Football League as a first-round draft pick: very rare. You need the right people to see you, and only then can the evaluation and "buzz" start about you. Always looms the possibility of a slow death as better players distract the scouts from your talent.

As I read the manuscript, I was overwhelmed with the passion and insightfulness it contained. I felt as if I were along a journey with a man as he matured and his perspectives changed.

As I showed it around, I always asked the same question, " Which poem is your favorite?" Had everyone come back with the response that a certain poem (or two) were their favorite, I would have come to the conclusion that the manuscript was essentially only a couple of good poems and filler. I was pleasantly surprised, however, as the responses returned with many different "favorites".

Poetry is a personal journey not only for the writer but also for the reader. As a reader reads, they will internalize and empathize with the writer and a connection will be made by the reader's past experiences and life. When different people, from different walks of life and of different ages, all come back with positive responses and have different favorites, the indication is that the manuscript is much more than "a couple of good poems with filler", but rather a very good quality manuscript. I agreed with the many responses and have my personal favorites (which are different from other people's).

As the book started to develop from the manuscript, things came together magically. A former Disney animator and published author jumped on board and then created illustrations from her interpretations of the poems. As I received these illustrations, I was amazed at the quality, not only of the illustrations themselves as illustrations, but also with the quality of the visualizations that came from the creativity of the illustrator.

I had always been a believer but that should never get in the way of objectivity from a business perspective. The many people that assisted in bringing this book from manuscript to reality have all been touched.

I believe you will also be touched. Join Derly Andre for a personal journey though 30 years of life. You won't be sorry that you did.

- Arnold G. Tijerina, III, publisher/editor, July 21, 2004

Table of Contents

Time of the Times..1

Daily Daze.. 3

Never Mind Time.. 5

Some Day's Dawn... 7

There Comes Upon a Time.. 9

Quotidian Quod.. 11

Later Retrieval.. 13

The Presence of Peace.. 15

Growing Up..17

Daily Fence... 19

Youth... 21

T'was the Night Before New Year's..23

Soul Searching..25

Ambition... 27

The Thin Grin.. 29

The Last Sweet Fruit of Summer...31

Dreams of Joseph... 35

Love..37

hopes & sparks..39

Waiting for a Loved One... 41

The Sound of Supper... 45

The Awaited Twinkle... 49

I Just Got the News.. 51

I Dare Anyone.. 55

Relationships..57

Panning for Gold... 59

Reflections.. 61

The Joys and the Beers... 63

A Scene in Harmony.. 65

Working Things Out.. 69

God & Me... 71

Women..**73**

    Fairy God Women... 75

    The Aura of Beauty... 79

    Tomorrow's Again.. 81

    Her Until.. 85

    Concerning Violence... 87

    Chit Chat.. 91

    Flustered Females.. 93

    Not Knowing... 95

Stuck or Lost...**97**

    A Diminished Echo... 99

    UNMIND... 101

    I Saw Jesus at the Grocery Store............................ 103

    Matter of Mind.. 107

    Surrounded... 109

    A Dog's Life.. 113

Sad Times...**115**

    Stuck or Standing... 117

    Trembling Within... 119

    Awakening... 123

    re-Awakening.. 124

    Collisions of Wealth and Woe................................ 127

    Confusion's Debris.. 131

    Pitter Patter... 135

Pneumatics...**137**

    The Seed Released... 139

    mosaics... 143

    OKAY... 145

    Coexistence... 147

    Silence.. 149

Time of the Times

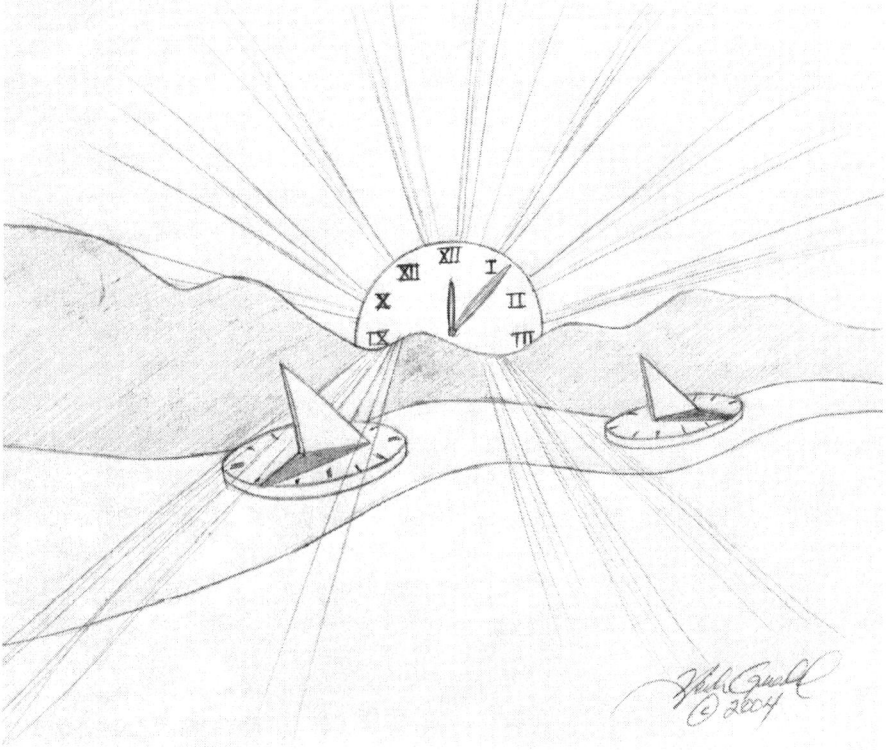

There is a relationship between a human consciousness and the stream of events that make up his or her life. That consciousness, like a passenger on a riverboat – that can only go downstream – sees things during a lifetime passing only once and forever. We drift by riverbanks of events that are components of our private beings.

When we consider one view of the riverbank, then another, we know time.

Daily Daze

I am sometimes fascinated by words that are entangled by sounds or meanings.
This poem is the result of noticing one day that "days" and "daze" can only
be distinguished in a sentence. The sounds that they share can only be
disentangled by a meaning derived from companions, much like friends or
memories.

Daily Daze

Waiting, wandering, I watch the days
in a daze that ascends from within,
where memories and meanings, descendants of time,
are tossed like sand in the wind.
They're incessantly coming and going again
to rest and be raised once more.
They're tumbled and churned toward another quick end,
a permanence known as a shore,
where feelings and thoughts lay side by side
composing great castles of sand.
They're fragile and futile but still fun to build
by accidents, each one unplanned.
And the day slips away or rushes right by
its vengeance and blessings unseen
while granular moments are buried or stacked
or perhaps just washed away clean.
Sands tear at my mind like wind to the blind
who can feel but see nothing defined.
It torments, resents, then quickly relents
and leaves scars, but no wounds behind.
And further and further time ticks away
while tomorrow comes and goes.
From whither to where? I continue to ask
but, alas, I can see know one knows!

-end-

Never Mind Time

I love Sunday naps. This was born in the wake of semi-consciousness, when dreaming, thinking and remembering are swirled into one thing and nothing matters.

Never Mind Time

It comes to mind on still night air,

on a Sunday nap or a day dream stare,

a moment so slyly escaping all care

that I find my never mind time.

As quiet and pure as one flake of snow

it silently twists and drifts by just so

that it creates its own glory, in a twinkle I know

the peace of never mind time.

Anxiously searching for glory or gold,

once plunged through childhood, man's hood grows old.

As for me, I don't search

I wait,

watch,

then hold,

the joy of my never mind time.

And the end we call death will eventually near

those contented, lamented – those with and without fear.

I privately expect that all things will be clear

in the stillness

of never mind time.

-end-

Some Day's Dawn

Weekdays are like the ticking of the corporate clock. Careers, families, circumstances grind through them like a millstone. Only a small amount of worthwhile essence is ever found in any one day. The catch is, you won't know that essence unless you are looking for it constantly.

Some Day's Dawn

A week of illusions come and gone
And over and over another dawn.
Faded feelings descend to where
Rising hopes still crowd the air.
Hopes are suspended by dreamy conceptions
That maturely awakens youth's self-deceptions.
The needed space never quite appears.
It keeps its distance. The dawn still nears.

And mighty men with their macho mirth
Continue the race renowned; the earth
While female halves wait or race,
But continue to drag at their self-set pace,
Seeking the half that resents the whole
And suspects possession of his freedomless soul.
Trapped between the days-long-past
And the tomorrow where all of his hopes are cast.
Freedom restrained by when and then
And the certainty of dawn tomorrow again.

Peace to each who seeks the time
As now preserved in a timid rhyme.

-end-

There Comes Upon a Time

The fleeting nature of each sensational event asks us to ponder. Among those things that flee are the thoughts and words, which can occasionally tumble together to form the harmony of rhyme carrying a tale.

There Comes Upon a Time

There comes upon a time in the evening
when minds are lightly at rest
and dreamy moods drift steadily
through moments preserved as "best."

They come and go with ease
like soft wind through golden-leafed trees
creating magical moments of mind
with perfect unintention designed.

Each leads nowhere but on to the next
when a determined mind is unflexed,
like a directionless breeze that stirs
a pure satin image of caresses like hers.

It's a mystery to me as they flow.
They can whisper, rush, linger, then go.
Like each silent breath used for rhyme
they light, just once, upon a time.

-end-

Quotidian Quod

Quod is a slang word used in Britain for prison. Next to it, in the dictionary, I discovered that 'quotidian' meant daily. Moments later, I was looking out at Friday afternoon traffic in Dallas, Texas from a sixth floor window. It was sometime around 1983.

Quotidian Quod

We race around to get ahead

our hearts and minds and souls are bled.

We try to gain or keep what's lost

among prisons of gold, the lives they've cost.

But we still are free to come and go

and the world's our playground

for use or show.

We show that loving and fighting are much the same.

the losers are hurt and the winners, win fame.

Fortune and fame, torture or shame,

needing and greeding and leading the game.

And round and round in a deadly race,

we continue to lose at a winning pace.

-end-

Later Retrieval

I wrote this in 1999, after I had been doodling with words for nearly 30 years. Like many of my pieces, the seed was the music in the first stanza, when some meaning is attached to a few words that produce a cadence that transcends the simple turn of a phrase. A melody with its own personality that sings of an emotional setting that is present at that moment. Moments like that yearn to be preserved.

Later Retrieval

I don't recall my face before wrinkles grew 'round my eyes
and I don't recall any thoughts that were innocent or unwise.

I only have some snapshots,
unsequential, unnumbered, unframed,
that were taken by a camera –
internal, well-focused, un-named.

Moments ordered by time pass by
undaunted by hopes or remorse
while smiles and laughter, pain and tears
ebb-and-flow as a matter of course
but through it all, the shudder might snap
on a sight, or a sound,
or a scent, or a thought.

Preserving forever in hallowed ground
images subtly stacked to profound
to be filed for later retrieval.

-end-

The Presence of Peace

My life is galvanized by a picture album, which records monumental tokens of love. In words, each picture tells a story set in time and each is fully infused with a sentiment that was rich at that very moment. In this snapshot, I recall a long moment in which a friend told me that "everything is going to be alright."

What was most interesting is that no one spoke. We had talked on the phone and I had shared the deep unsettling circumstances that brought me to my knees in confusion. All the facts were already on the table. Friend to friend, everything was understood.

So when we saw one another, there was only a hug.

The Presence of Peace

I have had occasion in my life to think on things that provide comfort in the midst of turmoil and confusion. Those thoughts often begin with musing on the opening line of the Desiderata, "Go placidly amid the noise and haste, and remember what peace there may be in silence." For when thoughts are rifling through my head, silence is like one card in a deck as they spill out of my hand onto the floor, where they lie in some random order.

When I find myself staring down at the unrelated mishmash of ideas that come out of confusion, like playing cards on the floor in an unnamed game, I can often find the flickering remnant of silence and the peace that it brings. It's not until I pick that one card up – the silent card – and think on it, that its monumental presence penetrates my being.

Once in a thoughtful moment like that, I came across the idea of the Apostle John laying his head onto the bosom of Jesus. I think about how the God of all humanity must have welcomed the young Apostle's gesture of affection. I put myself in John's place, young and admiring, in the presence of pure love and yet feeling pangs of the world in doubt and fear. I wonder about the physical sensation of the worn cloth on Jesus' robe and solid strength of the young carpenter's body (I have worked with thirty-year-old carpenters.)

In times of my deepest personal struggles, I hold a cartoon image of myself laying my own head in His bosom. He holds my head with both of his arms, just like my Mom did when I needed comfort as a child – a big strong active hug. Then the rest of the cartoon sketch has hurricane winds, flapping my body wildly like clothes outside on a clothesline caught by the wind that announces a thunderstorm. But my head is tightly snuggled into the comfort of the worn cloth and the boldness of His arms around my head.

From that position with my head (and mind) at rest and everything else about me flapping in the winds of change, I find the peace of silence. And in that silence I know that I am loved and that temporal things cannot infringe on that love.

So in silence, amidst the noise and haste, I do find peace in His grace. But the humanity of His touch is now left to the comfort of fellowship. And we take our turns, we need the comfort of our Christian brothers and sisters and we are asked, on occasion, to provide comfort for someone else in need. One who stands to console, and one who comes in need of comfort, stand eye to eye. We embrace.

And it's in the depth of the silence of the embrace that the gentlest encouraging words are whispered.

The day before Thanksgiving 2003 – caught in a windstorm and thankful for hugs.

Growing Up

I enjoy watching signposts on the way. They show you what's ahead. The trick is you rarely can read them, except when they are in the rear-view mirror. Ask any 18-year-old.

Daily Fence

For many years, writing poetry was a sporadic unintentional past time for me. I scratched at many things on many topics and only occasionally did a finished piece emerge from the tangle of thoughts, feelings, words and tinkling letters that fit together in patterns. Once in a while, out of the confusion, something would happen that brought very ordinary things into focus.

On one such occasion, I was sitting on a bench in my backyard and found a profound appreciation for the fact that I did not have to make any decisions on that particular day.

Daily Fence

decisions, decisions, decisions be gone.

your presence presents no peace.

annoyingly teetering on value's vague threads,

surmounting tangling, torturing dreads.

this way and that, all are wrong.

richness and wellness on no scale belong.

so weighted and hated is that indecisive song.

where melodies are vacant,

harmony can't exist

and playing strings of plenty

is menacing to resist.

so decisions guide us hither

they drive us on to naught

and slowly they recant to us

our destiny's end unsought

so, here I sit on weekday's bench,

where right and left are the same

and in my yard's daily fence

a deep sweet breath of indifference.

-end-

Youth

Brief is good – so is youth.

Youth

Steps were taken, the way passed by

day dreams drift, "good-times" fly

somewhere among moments highly strung

validity dawned and vanished young.

-end-

T'was the Night Before New Year's Eve

I like hanging out in coffee shops at bookstores, especially ones that keep AdBusters on the magazine rack. AdBusters is a funky mouthpiece for the graphical arts elitists, who fancy themselves way beyond ordinary coolness. In order to make that point perfectly clear, they compose ideas in taunt arrays of deliberate convocations; extreme post-modern graphical communications.

Once, they had an article about the Pope. It mentioned that he had noted a "crisis of meaning." Many, many months later I was in a conversation with my fourteen-year-old daughter and was longing for the airy philosophical conversations I used to have in my youth (hippy days). I tried to open a conversation about meaning and the potential for losing it. This is my venting in art when the effort crashed and burned and stunk like a fart at the altar.

I hated the fact that I had failed to introduce the joy of rhetoric to someone I loved so much.

T'was the Night Before New Year's

"Nihilism is at the root of the widespread mentality which claims that a definitive commitment should no longer be made, because everything is fleeting and ephemeral," the pope writes.

Nobody cares. It doesn't matter.

"As a philosophy of nothingness, it has a certain attraction for people of our time."

I don't want to think about it.

Why has the pursuit of meaning been abandoned? In part, the pope argues, because a dedication to human dignity is incompatible with the pure free market ethic of the post-totalitarian era.

What's meaningful to me
is not meaningful to you,
so why discuss it.

I just want to go shopping.

"No less pernicious, though not always as obvious, are the effects of materialistic consumerism,

What really hurts
is that you don't
understand lip gloss . . . that's
meaningful.

in which the exaltation of the individual and the selfish satisfaction of personal aspirations become the ultimate goal of life," he declared this New Year's Day.

Don't you get it?
I just want to have fun without
having to think.
It's New Year's Eve
(. . . you pathetic dweeb.)

"In this outlook, the negative effects on others are considered completely irrelevant."

You're the one who's miserable.

Can I have my ride now,
my friend is waiting.

-all quotes from AdBusters – Oct 2001-

Soul Searching

I have been an amateur philosopher since I was 18 years old. I flew through Ayn Rand, Carlos Castenadas, Herman Hesse, the Baghava Gita, the Koran, the I Ching. Add Transcendental Meditation, a week and a half with Hare Krishna, brushes with Tantric Yoga, Kabala, astrology and Ekencar and the notion of destination, journey and travel become as clear as puke after a chili cook off.

Amidst all the wanderings, there was a constant harmony between thoughts of the soul and the physics of light.

Soul Searching

i was wandering alone
in search of my soul
when a vacancy dawned,
like an eye's pupil - a whole.

a vacuum drew me in
retrospecting, reflecting, unchanged
silent harmonies were scattered
but the wholeness was not rearranged.

in solitude it stood
absent of all thought
like a star-spangled night of plenty
by no camera can ever be caught

as darkness eludes the light
and the truth inhibits our sight
a dream can bless us with flight
and my soul, just a void, shines delight.

-end-

Ambition

This is based on a true incident. I was driving a Ford F-150 pick up truck,
as my rugby days faded into a career in sales. As I was trying to get to an
appointment one morning, a three-inch grasshopper showed up in the cab of
my truck. When I noticed it at the stop light, I watched it as it would try to
launch into, what seemed to be, the open air but which was actually the glass of
the windshield. The strength and energy he put into his flailing was admirable.

Ambition

on my way to an early appointment,
dreaming about ambition
and sleepy through the traffic
populated with wealth's admonition.
if I ever owned a Cadillac,
would I still want to drive a jag?
and would haunting chemical dependency
still, like a ball-and-chain, drag?

but thoughts like that are infrequent.
I still have a job to do.
no damage is done by directionless dreams.
events of today help me through.

then, damn it, a grasshopper, caught in the car
out of reach, on the dash, where he sat
so he flailed while I waited for the light to change
and I witnessed ruthless combat.
again and again, at the window, he lunged
undaunted by pain or fatigue.
I studied and envied its tireless fire
his determination piqued intrigue.

so late or not, i pulled off the road
near a field, i unbuckled my belt
and reaching across – hot coffee in my lap
its sting, sharp irony felt.

my lofted ambitions were no plight to him
as for dreams, he didn't need 'em
and free-fluttering wings sang loud in my heart
for (like me) he just needed freedom.
-end-

The Thin Grin

There is a lonely, yet captivating cycle attached to beer drinking. It always starts with anticipation. Friday nights used to hold so much promise, until of course, you discover that the pattern of disillusion, then disappointment, then blur, then morning after hangovers filled with both physical and emotional litter.

This was a moment on the cusp of understanding. There was a hint of the urge to get out of the cycle . . . but not just before happy-hour.

The Thin Grin

Wisdom speaks but only few hear
Through whispers and tears, grins and beers

A cloud that clutters the dim sky,
later glows with the sunset
and like a torch in the human spirit,
that single cloud entrances a mind so unsure.

It whispers timeless colorful light.
It tastes of yesterday's tart sweetness
Enticing remote lonely stares.

The end of the stare ignites the thin grin,
Which evolves to a smile,
Then a laugh . . .
all within.

It starts, flows and flashes
Like my thirty-three years
And the rest still
Excites me, like Friday-night beers.

-end-

The Last Sweet Fruit of Summer

I loved every minute of my rugby career. I began to play when I was twenty and lived on the East coast. I played my last game at thirty-five. At one point, I attempted a summer comeback after recovering from an injury late in my career. I went to an ordinary practice and on an ordinary play, which should never have harmed anyone, an odd thing happened. A combination of a fall that should have turned easily into a shoulder roll and a vigorous push from an opponent caused me to fall awkwardly on my shoulder. The force of the impact and the severe lack of drama in the play made it almost embarrassing to admit that I had been hurt, but I was. I had to leave the practice. As I drove away, my career flashed before my eyes.
So many years of frolic . . . now gone.

The Last Sweet Fruit of Summer

I remember when the blossoms
were radiant laurels of spring,
the fruit had not yet teased my mind
intently as eagle's still wing.
my heart was tainted with youth
and bellowed each hopeful song
while dreams both hither and yon could fly
not knowing my place to belong.

but as the fruit started its colorful life
I stayed where I wanted to be
in sun or shade, both wet and dry
provided by this matronly tree
I'd gorge on fruit with mindless bliss
its sweetness never paled
and the demise of hunger's bittersweet pang
had never, not once, ever failed.

so the summer passed, while i on my back
lazily reached out a hand
and the most ripened fruit dropped neatly in
such accidents couldn't be planned
with a belly full I'd let them fall
each rotting for the seed's sake
and napped to contentment, I lofted sweet dreams
no value in being awake.

con't

one day, whenever, I opened one eye

outstretched, my hand was unfilled.

a deep green hue and breeze passed by,

the summer had sailed on unwilled.

the fruit on the tree was scarce.

the earth now nursed fruit which had perished.

canned or jarred, the fruit's not as sweet,

like youth photographically cherished.

leaping and scratching for fruit didn't help.

a slumber laden body can't provide.

and blissful ignorance in the sun and the shade

is now irreversibly denied.

so off to work, and growth, and mirth,

man's hood grows familiar to me.

and I've noticed a fruit, I forgot once to eat

has grown, now a fruit bearing tree.

the tree's bold young branches are growing with ease

nourished by effortless time,

the fruit's not yet ripened and won't drop with haste,

each drops at a time pre-assigned,

like moments of blessing and moments of doom,

in rhythm can never be traced

and autumn's arrival shows colors and hues

harmony poetically laced.

-end-

Dreams of Joseph

Careers are like epic mini-series, such as Roots. They cross boundaries of decades and stages of life that never align well with steps taken, stumbling blocks and set backs.

Throughout it all, there are hopeful moments in which youthful anticipations seem to (almost) line up with the reality of a workday situation.

But most days present a distinct mismatch between what is and what was "supposed to be".

Dreams of Joseph

I think I've reached a stage.

There's something broad and flat

beneath me, it . . .

It's just wider than my view from here

in the midst of my life.

I can study it,

but it slides ahead of me

at exactly the same rate as I am stepping.

So it is never exactly clear

if I have completely reached the stage,

or if perhaps,

it is the next step that

will signal

the heralding

that will be announced

as foretold

in the fortune teller's tale, whispered in youthful praise.

I dimly remember . . . back then, I was promised

the heralding trumpets and the monogrammed

doilies from the office parties.

"Your superiors will bow to your wisdom,

like the dreams of Joseph."

But no!

The spotlight's over there.

-end-

Love

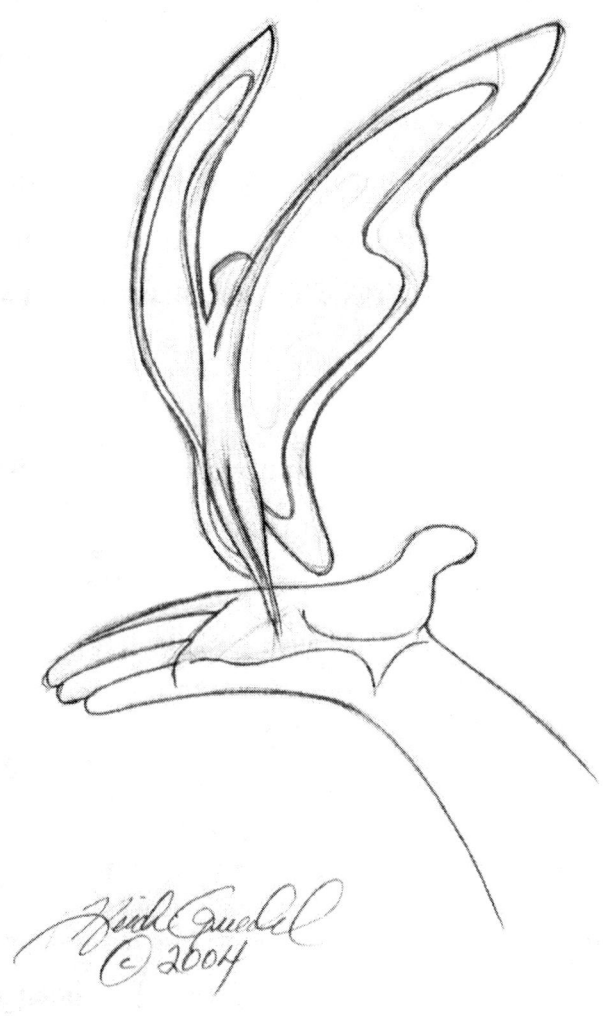

My view is limited – my interest keen.

hopes & sparks

A roller coaster ride can't be any good without height and speed, neither
can love. Implied in that ride are times that are slow. Reminiscing takes on
different tones like the hues of a sunset. They transform images of the past into
thoughts that are only sometimes comprehensible.

hopes & sparks

I stagger among memories

emotional remnants

of shattered romance

and search for those moments of peace

where slight hopeful smiles

were accented by the corners of her eyes

just so.

monuments of pain

tarnished, benign

stand

so still

like statues in the park

casting shadows from time to time.

yet the hope in her eyes

deny any damage is real.

a bosom intent is content.

hope drains.

sparks burn.

a lonely moment holds both.

-end-

Waiting for a Loved One

I used to love to pick my wife up at Austin's Mueller airport after her business trips. She mostly flew Southwest Airlines and we both enjoyed the consistency of the rhythm in which they performed their duties. They were not always on time, but they handled things in a consistent manner whether it was good news (your plane has just arrived, we will be departing in fifteen minutes) or bad news (we have no idea how late your plane will be, but for this announcement we are going to tell you it will be fifteen minutes longer - so you won't get mad right now).

I enjoyed waiting and watching the people.

Waiting for a Loved One

Waiting for a loved one . . .

a tapping foot addendum
to a mourningful clock, so still
and a pounding heart subdued
by a patient concerted will.

The time won't pass. It stands.

so a mind full wanders by and by
and clouds not moving clear the sky
the aching void unfilled won't die
when alone, not abandoned, one mustn't cry.

Even endless waiting can't last.

hopeful reminiscence of times now gone
distort all movement and sound
while ritual wanting to exercise love
lets grounded feelings rebound

Because the loved one will certainly return.

so swift sure efforts
are worked towards connection
and absolved separation
will dismiss feared rejection.

con't

So a load is lightened standing at journey's end.

somehow perched on the horizon

the unapproaching time is now here

the loved one displaced for that eon

has returned reflecting needs to be near.

The first touch ends separation

so the kiss can send hearts soaring home.

-end-

The Sound of Supper

My wife has a great aunt that continued producing original works of art into her ninetieth year. I shared some of my poetry with her and one evening, when she and I were alone, she said that she had always loved the time spent after supper, talking and visiting with good friends or family. She asked me specifically if I might be able to write a poem about those times.

I took months and months to think about it and had almost given up when I noticed one evening with family that there was a unique combination of sounds that occurred after supper. People came and went at a different pace and dishes were shuffled while the main attraction was derived from the range of emotions that were shared among those who sat and remained at the table. My Aunt Elizabeth enjoyed this poem and I had to include my own Mom and her sister (Alma and Gloria) as thinking about such times is fused in my memory with their laughter.

The Sound of Supper

We feed each other as we are fed
and minds stay opened, as our hearts are bled.
we savor the words that each has said,
as the sound of supper goes down.

We take deep breaths and sigh relief.
We discuss, we argue, we share disbelief
in what has become of our fathers' grief,
as the sound of supper goes down.

Like the sun of sunrise, or the sound of a dawn,
people surround us - where we are, we belong
and we sip from the love of sweet memory's song,
as the sound of supper goes down.

My back's not as strong as it used to be,
but my eyes are sharp, I know what I see,
like high notes and low notes in harmony
are the sounds of supper going down.

When Elizabeth and Alma and Gloria sit still,
tears and tales and laughter thrill
as their lives have unfolded and God had His will
and resounded by things going down.

con't

The sound in the corners of their eyes as they smile,

the sound of patience through the length of the mile,

youthful styles, defy denial,

at their best when supper goes down.

For food is abundant but love is not

good food and good love on one plate are brought

like the smell of good coffee or a long distance thought

when the sound of supper goes down.

It fades, and blends but never really ends

into sounds of activities or laughter with friends.

I savor the memories, love makes amends

as the sound of supper goes down.

Every meal has its day

and loving cooks pass away,

recorded here to replay

all the sounds of those suppers gone down . . .

mmmmmmm . . .

-end-

The Awaited Twinkle

There's nothing more nourishing to a relationship than to say, "I love you."
Unless, of course, it is the deep instinctual reaction that the loved one creates in
a secret "twinkle" that issues back to the lover. A simple and perfect full round
trip; said, heard, understood.

The Awaited Twinkle

again and again and again.

it sounds awkward and useless to know

and yet in that rhythm

there is captured

a rare and wonderful treasure

that becomes itself only in passing.

it lingers and makes senses

reach toward fulfillment.

while knowing all along

that the moment just gone by

will remain as is, hopelessly unattainable,

but certainly must still be framed

to preserve that magical moment

with all of its bittersweet views.

while emotional hues rinse the bejeweled facts

as they evolve into polished heartfelt memories

like the one now ascending.

it drenches the present.

you're gone, but recreated

in my mind.

your smile,

    your sad knowing eyes,

       and the twinkle

          when I say, "i love you!"

-end-

I Just Got the News

The happiest thing about New Year's 2000 was that I no longer had to be a man of the 90's. That tag was so heavily laden with mixed messages, that I openly joked about my glee.

But through the nineties I grew as a Dad and learned to know parenting from the inside out. Then, as the decade drew to a close, my Mom died after a long drawn out illness. My business meetings had to continue immediately after the funeral and I was caught off guard more than once when grief struck like a thunderbolt in the middle of the business day. I wanted to cry in the open, because most people knew about my loss. But still, it just was not socially acceptable.

All grief and social progress for women aside, I could not bear the cost of crying, even when consumed with legitimate grief. One day, two weeks after she died, I wrote this about the struggle.

I Just Got the News

my umbrella won't open

and my sunscreen's gone dry

there's a hole in my mit

and sand in my eye.

i'm a man of the nineties,

so i'm glad i can cry.

i just got the news . . . my Mom died.

at forty-plus years

i've had plenty of beers

i've loved and lost

i know stupidity's cost

i've played with pain

and been tipped toward insane

i've been stuffed in the dirt

but i never knew hurt.

i just got the news . . . my Mom died.

it's a brick in the head

and a slow dance with dread

it's cheers and a hoot

digging memory's loot

it's a scream in the wind

and a hug with a friend

con't

it's "eewh" and it's "ouch"

and long stares on my couch

i just can't quite know

when the whirlwind will slow

i just got the news . . . my Mom died.

i can't touch her hand

but i remember it well

it was strong and kind

and could pinch like hell

she had cooked and had cleaned

her fingers to the bone

my messes and hunger

like the seasons had flown

now i harvest the thoughts

and regret lots of oughts

i just got the news . . . my Mom died.

i once knew a kid who watched his Dad drown

and i'm embedded with a melody called "tears of a clown"

i knew a few orphans

and i've looked into coffins

but i never understood,

no one ever could,

believe wholeness was punctured

like a swim with a two-ton lanyard

con't

i just got the news . . . my Mom died.

in fatigue my tears can flow

when i'm in meetings, i can't let it show

nineties or not

you just can't get caught

with feelings in-the-raw

(a societal flaw)

no, i just look away

vote yeah or nay

get back to the grind

get "it" off my mind

you see, it's been two weeks

she's buried and gone, but

i just GOT the news . . . my Mom died.

-end-

I Dare Anyone (1972)

To my best recollection, this is the first poem I ever wrote. I had a neighbor/
friend/lover/counselor once. At age eighteen, I wrote this about how she was
entwined in my life.

I Dare Anyone

I dare anyone

    to stand between the cool of night, and

    the crispness of the dawning day, or

    to feel the heat of the rising sun

    and ignore the new lit sky.

I dare anyone

    to call my breath separate from the wind, or

    to prevent a tear from melting into infinity.

I dare anyone

    to tell me that the rhythm of

    your heartbeat is unrelated to

    the harmony in my soul, or

    that heaven begins only where

    the sky ends.

I dare anyone

    to draw a line between me and you, or

    to refuse our outstretched hands, and

    ignore the love and understanding that they offer.

If anyone can,

    then I must leave them in their

    victorious ignorance and their lonely misunderstanding . . .

    forever with the patient company of my hope.

-end-

Relationships

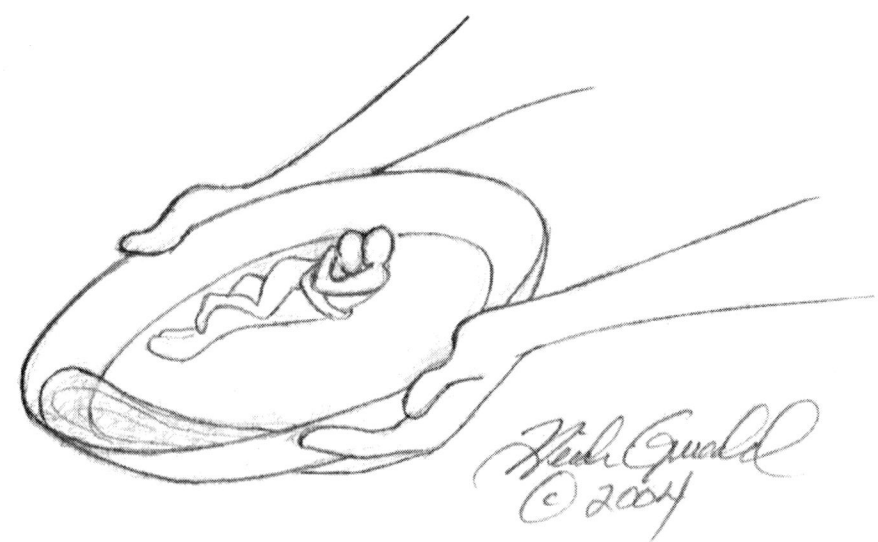

Of all great mysteries, there are none so incomprehensible as when two people truly fall in love.

Panning for Gold

There was a hot rock-and-roll club in Dallas in the late 70's and into the first few years of the 80's called St. Christopher's. It was known for live music seven nights a week. Stevie Ray Vaughn was among the regulars on weeknights as he made his way between Denton and Austin for weekend gigs.

It was a long narrow room and the stage backed up to Greenville Ave. In a few parking spaces just outside the club, you could look all the way through the bar. You could see the back of the band as they played and then you could only see shapes in the crowd, where it was dark, but you could detect the motion and the energy among the sweaty bodies. Way behind all the people, from that vantage point, was the bar. It was also lit. From one of those parking spaces, I sat in my pick-up truck. I could see the silhouettes of the people who were in need of one more beverage. The heat in the place was intense on many levels. I wrote this while watching the scene.

Panning for Gold

All the lost souls were panning for gold

Among the noise and the smoke and the hot rock-and-roll

Elbow-to-elbow they pushed for more

Intoxicant treasures and pleasures galore

Willing to wait in confusion's debris

Of glances, chances, romances to be

Hoping for more than those other nights

Seeking specific enchanting delights

The men and the women are all the same

Sure of their change of luck in the game

Cute couples stayed

While the music played

And singular dreams were lost or delayed

Smiles shined brightly in drunken styles

And shattered hopes made neat lonely piles

And eyes closed wide

To feelings inside

All were lustful and eager to be glorified

While the night waned away

Towards another today

All were excited and hid their dismay

And tomorrow did come

Embracing new fun

And lost souls continued right where they'd begun.

-end-

Reflections

This is a 1999 tale of a quiet moment on a pleasant night. I was in Eau Claire, Wisconsin, a petite healthy mid-western community, by myself reviewing all that I had to be thankful for.

Reflections

I like to remember things I've done
the good, the bad, the unclean
then I'm burned by the power, the heat of the sun,
a scorching light, pure but unseen

it captures my mind
sorts things by their kind
go forward, leave some things behind,
act like the blind,
don't seek or find.
await things blessed . . . divined.

I am happy to write
and I am happy to see
I ponder on things in reflection

lights shine on
old lovers are gone
and my life is now filled with perfection.

-end-

The Joys and the Beers

I have two daughters and we have friends who have a family with four boys.
Their mom and my wife knew each other as singles and we have all been
friends since the oldest of the children was a baby. When boyish ways meet
girlish charm in the protection of innocence, there is an interchange that is
not unlike a 1950's musical. Kids do numbers in different configurations and
once in a while, a solo will steal the show. In the midst of the excitement is an
underlying issue . . . boys and girls are different.

The Joys and the Beers

Boys must be boys

and girls must have curls . . .

so hard action toys

battle flirtatious noise

and parents rejoice at momentary joys.

Each must have their time to play

and yesterday remembers the tomorrow delay . . .

growth by the minute, growth by the year

time rumbles on like a trickling tear

and energy flows like the head on a beer.

Toys and noise

and years and tears,

all summed up are

the joys and the beers.

-end-

The Scene in Harmony

Performing arts are shared in all cultures of all continents throughout all time. When people share time together with music and divide into performers and listeners. They are linked by a complex of sound in a specific setting.
A community speaks and responds to notes and voices that are arranged to replay thoughts written in some other time and place. In worship, a remarkable church choir, told me this secret.

A Scene in Harmony

the air and the light and the music were hung

like a mural on the wall

and voices entwined in harmonies

drenched my mind like a mirrored hall

high notes and low notes in melodies

danced like a fiddler's tune

and stained glass colors shined out loud

when harmonies lit the room

each voice was strong in agreed upon keys

while the time of day cast the sunlight

and hearts communed beyond what man sees

like wind lifts the bird – still-winged flight

one voice can't make a choir

one note can't make a tune

one word can't make a poem

and later can't stand without "soon"

but together voices can harmonize

creating new peace in new hearts

and on brilliant days in sunlit ways

choirs can throw off love's sparks.

con't

some notes are sounded while others are sung

and the air is filled where silence was hung

in stanzas and stillness harmony rings

coupled with patterns like colors dawn brings

one note alone, like only one hue,

can't do by themselves what harmonies do

a blend or contrast that makes two things one

creates a new being, and additive sum.

one voice can't make a choir

one note can't make a tune

one word can't make a poem

and later can't stand without "soon"

harmony lives in relations, which surround us in all our days

and love aches to know beauty in her mysterious ways

while we turn our heads toward material dreads

we see today and tomorrow as odd newlyweds

it makes no sense, this harmony,

to exist when only between

things set in themselves, to be what they are,

so a soul can reflect what's been seen.

-end-

Working Things Out

As a student of human nature, I love to ponder relationships among not only individuals, but institutions, organizations and cultures. This piece is about the pervasive frustration I find in things planned centrally, by the federal government and the realities of commerce in everyday life.
For some reason, the notion of castle walls and serfdom and peasant merchants dealing with one another rang out in my mind.

Working Things Out

Once upon a time, in a fertile land, rich with commerce, giants built magic castles to protect the people's riches. The castle's walls were strong and high. The gates were kept closed and drawbridges were needed to cross moats built to guarantee the safety of the community wealth, and the royal court, of course. Common people paid tax there – the farmers, craftsmen and merchants, alike. And only the royal court could hand out goods from the storehouses or provide services. Only they could give access to grains and materials used by the craftsmen and offered by the merchants.

A sleep fell over the royal court. The guard still stood day and night. They kept the drawbridge greased; the gates in working order and the motes clear of debris (lest someone might cross.) The people clamored for services outside the castle's walls but sometimes the bridge was drawn up. Other times, the gate was only partially opened, so only a few could be served. And still other times (when things *were* open) all the people couldn't fit on the bridge and through the gate when they wanted to cross.

The guards announced more bridges would be built. More gates have been planned. The moat will be filled. But alas, the royal court slept.

The youth of the land didn't remember when the castle was built (or why). So, in the streets and the markets, they began to offer services of their own. They no longer stored grain inside the castle walls that the bakers needed to fetch. They shared available space and resources and talents. And the fertile fields prospered. Craftsmen produced and merchants thrived.

The guards still stood, day and night. Bridges and gates and moats, were all in order. They kept their trumpets polished. Bright banners waved high when the new gates were opened and additional bridges were built. All the people would pause and listen to the ancient sounds of self-absorption.

But they went back about their business sharing and prospering . . . because it worked.

-end-

God & Me

The more directly God is approached with words, the more He evades definition.

God & Me

i understand   He loves

i see   He lives

i speak   He compels

i both follow and lead   He is

i am   we are

and   so are you.

- (HIS) ends (ONLY) -

Women

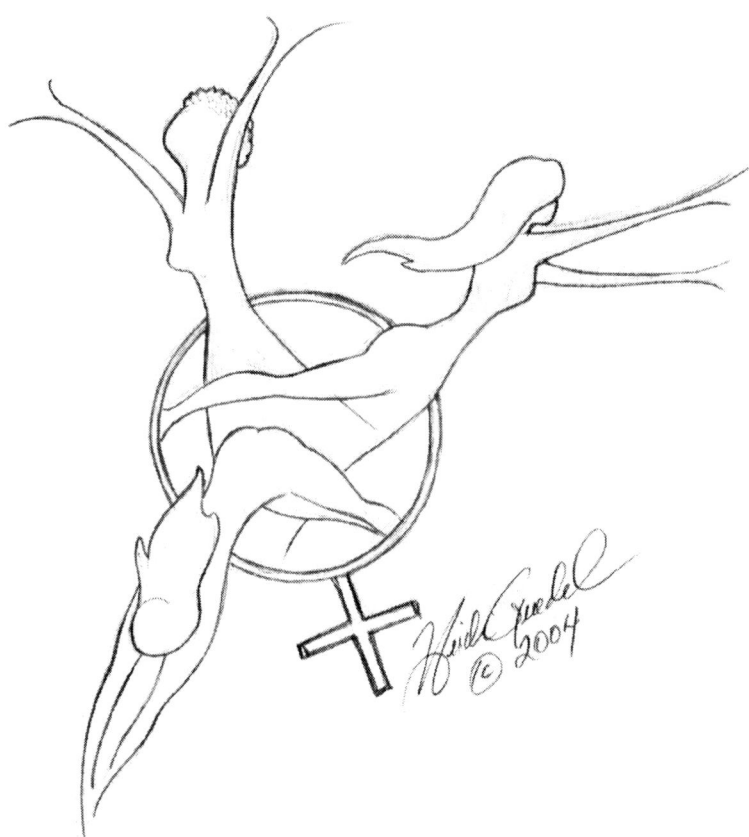

I have written mostly about women who are perplexing or who appear (to me) to be perplexed. The powerful, lost, the lonely and confused were all fascinating human adventures as I wormed my way out of my own extended adolescence. Of all things, I admire the zeal that is exercised on both sides of the emotional volley. One can only stand in reverent awe at the spectrum of femininity.

Fairy God Women

As we were going to press in the Fall of 2004, I felt somehow uneasy about the overall composition of this section. I know so many women who are admirable just in being themselves – they are not as much perplexed as they are fully engaged in life. When I see each of them in their own personal little moments of exuberance, I notice a twinkling that reminds me of the magical saviors of Disney fame, like Cinderella's Fairy God Mother or Pinnochio's Blue Fairy. In their ordinary moments, I call these women my Fairy God Women. As I complete this piece in January 2005, I now submit my book as complete.

Fairy God Women

My mind is full of lovely thoughts

The many women I've known.

I ponder each element of the landscape

Each with its own grandeur and place.

For feminine elements glimmer with scents

That reflect emotional notes

. . . secret notes.

Those thoughts twinkle with personality

Style and shape and tone and texture

They play harmony and charades, solo and in chorus

So very different and all the same . . . women.

Deluxe in variety, marching band noise, daily deliberations, cherishing youth

Yet each is directly engaged in the turmoil of today

The 'woulds' and 'shoulds' battle the 'would've' and 'could've.'

The 'would've' curves in and each 'could've' was clear,

like romantic adventures or bubbles in beer.

And deep from within ancient eternal femininity

notices the unicorn of her own private perhaps.

Wild, untamed and shy

The giant gentle beast, sleeps like a child on a summer lawn,

drunk on grassy green.

It is still and safe near the creek,

asleep, this unicorn dreams of her secret notes.

The fairy in every Fairy God Woman twinkles and twists,

like when the belle of the ball was called Tinker.

What did Tinkerbell do anyway? She flits around dying for attention and all the while willing to lay down her life to save the one she unconditionally loves. Meanwhile, he (PeterPan) goes about his adventure doing what's right with panache and cleverness.

Pirate's ships and mermaid lagoon,

Wendy and swords and shadows she couldn't mend

(. . . that was Wendy's job.)

Each of my Fairy God Women is like one unique set of ripples

that shimmer in a long stemmed wine glass,

especially when someone laughs too hard.

Humming in that glass of wine is a glimpse of crimson clarity. God's fruit reflects the laughter covering the shared air – the wine, she and me – I pause to consume that moment of grace.

I like the wine.

I like the laughter.

But it is the fairy – shimmering – that makes my life worthwhile.

She is my wife, my mother, my sister

She is my daughter, my niece, and my aunts

She smiles at PTA meetings and loads a suburban with Texan charm.

I've seen her without makeup on mission trips,

And I've hugged each in the halls of our church.

I coffee, I lunch, and pray in small groups

We share our families and the strength of our love

But always hook up on what's from above.

I taught their sons and daughters in Sunday School

and drove designated driver for their son's bachelors party.

(The love of wedding should not be dampened by the fear of poor judgment.)

It was God's hand that brought us all together in ways only she can understand.

Each child, each man, each pain, each worry,

each unique, each in a perfect place, to be

so that each woman

　　will never by like every woman.

That's where God's part of Fairy God Women comes in.

Like the stars of heaven each woman has a place in the universe.

A place that no one else in all history can fulfill.

Other people will navigate off that star . . . each star.

So I watch the constellations of women in full gear

and stand in awe at the depth and degree of glimmering purity –

the spectrum of femininity.

Fairy God Women of my soul,

shimmer boldly in your own private path,

so that we adventuring flittering boys can navigate

each time we are privileged to hear long enough to catch the scent of secret notes.

The only thing I can offer – each and every one of my Fairy God Women is honor.

I am honored to know your blessings.

Derly Andre

(after serving breakfast tacos to the Honduras Mission Team – January 22, 2005)

The Aura of Beauty

Long ago I understood the distinction between women who are striking and
women who are truly beautiful. It is almost an inside-out sort of relationship.
Striking is all intended to be for others to observe. Beauty is something deep,
internal and constant, beyond such temporary things as bad hair days.

The Aura of Beauty

there's something chemical about beauty,

like a scent or a taste.

beauty announces itself with an aura of stillness

that dominates even a noisy room.

it's beyond good looks, or even striking style,

it's more potent.

for you see, beauty includes a plumb-line of truth

that says things that 'should be'

are perfectly aligned with the things that 'are'.

when a woman grows into her own beauty,

there's a harmony in the stillness she sends into the air,

for any who are willing to listen.

the chatter of fakery and painted lost hope

are denied their voices for many clear moments,

just as beauty enters awareness . . . then,

beauty is present,

the way God asked it to appear.

let the willing listen

so God can bless those who can tune their senses
toward the mysterious;

like the sound of a scent,

or the texture on a taste.

the aura of beauty is the nectar of a prepared mind.

-end-

Tomorrow's Again

Like "Panning for Gold", this story was written about an event that occurred at St. Christopher's on Greenville Avenue in Dallas around 1982, I was 26. I was working at St. C's as a bar-back, pouring beer and wine, keeping ice and beer mugs stacked and watching the world go by.

One evening, I was lured to an after party (at about 2:30am) with co-workers and a 'few' clients. The one who had invited me was attractive and feminine, dark hair and blue eyes. She had been in the bar most of the night but was only a moderate drinker, as far as I could tell. I was thoroughly interested – until, that is, I learned she was fifteen years old.

I left abruptly and went to an all-night diner to wrestle with the impact of such deception. I wrote "Tomorrow's Again" because she was in such a hurry to beat a game she didn't understand. When I gave this to her the next week, she went into the bathroom and cried.

I was berated by her friend for my brutality even though she hadn't read the poem at that point. She was twenty years old (also too young to be in the bar).

Tomorrow's Again

Moving with ease that wind does blow

and its restlessness is comfort

'cause it just wants to go.

No matter, no mind, but power to spare.

It's rough, tough and timid

in its stillness, just air.

But stirred into motion it'll tease and break trees

and the power of God makes high winds or breeze.

with fine fluid motions she flows through the room

and the future's inside her concealed in her womb.

hoping to be something she's not

illusions, confusions, conclusions untaught.

still eager to master the mystery of men,

her youth's her worst weapon, for it sets the trend,

while hoping and groping for what's yet to come

she forgets to remember that she's still under thumb,

pinned by the teachings and preachings of men,

she twists and she squirms against tomorrow's again.

she tries to be wise with maturely closed eyes

and the feelings are borrowed like odd eager sighs.

the reach for tomorrow is what creates sorrow

and touchings and feelings are sad things to borrow,

because pay back she will for each sigh and thrill,

she'll be lost in the morning with longing to kill.

kill the pain of the memory, hopelessly sensory,

created by men, again and again.

con't

With patience and presence it flows to the sea

for its direction is set and clear.

All water is ready to move soft and steady

towards the only goal it knows.

It seeks the center without any mentor

it just feels for downward then flows.

And reaching its end, it is sent back again

to drift upward and onward and come back one then.

but a woman in love with one man is neat

she uses, abuses, then toys with her treat.

until finally she sees that the results of her tease

are her own loving, caring and needing to please.

now, quite confused, she reaches for more.

she'll create a child, a son to adore.

she'll pay him with time, endlessly spent.

the changings, the feedings, are no more than rent,

for his time will come to learn to run.

tears burden her eyes as she says her good-byes,

just-friends, just-teachers, just-girls are all lies.

what seems to be, is what is and what goes.

the pain of the truth, she'll feel as he grows.

in the end, he's a man, and after then's then

she'll painfully see it's tomorrow's again.

The wind and the rain don't know pleasure or pain

so comfort is a matter of course

and maidens still seek strong pride turned to meek –

the magic enchantment of the single-horned horse.-

-end-

Her Until

I was sitting by myself at a table for two, facing the entrance of a nice business-lunch place in Dallas. People entering the room were two steps higher than the floor where the tables were. As I sat about ten feet from that rise my eye level was at the knees of people coming in – it was rather uncomfortable. One young woman in her mid-twenties told me this tale as she waited to be seated

Her Until

Don't look at me

I'm not special

It makes me mad

My eyes aren't blue

And my hair's not long

I didn't have time

to do my nails

or notice my hem

is falling.

Don't look at me

I'm not wearing the right makeup

it's all I had

I saw some in a magazine that

would be better.

it highlights!

When summer comes, I'm going

to lose weight

and get a tan.

I have a friend who

said she would teach me

to dance, too

but until then . . .

-end-

Concerning Violence

I have known more than just a few powerful women. I was educated and shaped by things I learned from them. As a rugby player and philosopher, I contemplated many things to many depths. Among them, competition and violence. Competition and violence, as known on the rugby field, exist on a plane above twentieth century America. There is a timeless quality to the purity of such combat and I knew it well.

But there are other forms of violence that manifest in comparable sequences of jabs and right hooks. I wrote this after being beaten and kicked. The magnitude of the intent was what made me hurt.

In some ways, I don't like the way this particular poem turned out. It approaches the degree of confusion and lostness I felt. But, it does not clearly state how vicious it felt. I have known the fist of a 250lb angry man – it was my right cheek and it bled . . . this was worse.

Concerning Violence

suddenly he found himself lost
among familiar scenes
looking at their knees
a twisting hair-bow, on a knee, a dip of the head
a woeful silence in the air.

misunderstood, no, misunderstanding
in process could stand no longer.
strength in a field of men was clear,
a fist, a glance, then détente.
and violence for fun (to play in the mud)
like boys (God forbid) worse than lust

so doting mothers, tossed pigtails,
giggling teens, save-the-gay-whales
walk and strut, glare and smile
with carnivorous hopes, each their own style.
they plea with silence and pry with perfection
until they state their case with feline inflection
because each and every is justified
when they see a man's ego
so keenly denied.
pride, no pride, pride, no pride.

slight humilities like grandma's grin
rise like bubbles - champagne in a tin.
a feigned imitation of grandmother's grace
they've found good footing in an uneven race
and they never are seen in a pink bow or lace.

no these are new women.

success is camouflaged with brand-name-tags

airline tickets and shopping bags

while Grecian dreams like a ball-and-chain drags

but the battlefield is set, the rules are clear

(unspoken, vague, democratic, no fear)

"I learned from a pro to get what I want" she was such a
noble person,

well maybe, so-what,

"but my dad always told me -

but I can't remember why,

"and that arrogant son-of-a-bitch will never make *me* cry.

he's slick and he's showy and he screwed up my dreams."

and her shipwrecked-spent confidence, denies what it seems

all is damaged in her sight -

like caterpillars denied their flight.

the struggle is quiet, but also fierce and real

and words are no match for those stainless looks of steel.

so a warrior of old in a frightening fray

has no claws, no weapons, nothing left to say,

deep apologies moan and swell in his chest

when standing understood

(no really just jest)

my error so clear

it will never happen again . . .

for today,

i've felt

. . . in your silence,

a feminine

form of violence.

-end-

Chit Chat

This is one of those pieces I found in my desk. I remember very little about the situation except that very young mothers were chatting vigorously about their babies (the oldest were toddlers). There were lots of exclamations and biz bang stories flying.

Oddly enough, the only thing I remember clearly was that the mothers had finger nail polish jobs that were distinctly adolescent. Nails were obviously bitten to the nub, then they were painted and left unattended for long enough to be spotty, much like what I associate with freshmen girls in high school.

There was lots of noise (and they were smoking) as they watched their kids.

Chit Chat

chit chat chit chat

nag nag nag

blah blah blah

zig zig zag

cough cough, choke choke

drip fly drag

whiz bang spew choke

wave, signal, flag

whew, wow, howdy boy

a message heard, a horse from Troy

[sleeping among the linguistics – guttural rhythmic joy]

tempered both by attitudes and nails gnawed off, then polished

the youthful mothers conversed with innocence just now abolished.

each had her story

– as did mine –

and mothers always will

whimsically banter details told

'bout a God-given infant thrill.

-end-

Flustered Females

I have done many miles in the air for business travel. In all my travels there is a ubiquitous persona. It is the female traveling professional. This is a note that I jotted down after overhearing a long lunch worth of anecdotes from a table where four such women shared their woes.

I will apologize in advance, in case anyone takes offense to this piece. Sometimes I hear a turn of a phase in my head and I write it down before I unravel any other dimensions.

Flustered Females

flustered females to and fro,

the men can't get what the men don't know

the pace of the race is go-wait-stop-go

while the men bet themselves to win, place or show

all cast their dreams on the fiddler's tune.

some like pleasure-island, others mermaid lagoon.

caught in their dreams-of-fancy, like air in a balloon.

it's counted late, if done on time, but never can be too soon

men deprived by the power of X

might stand for one and succumb to the next.

slaughtered by dreams he never elects,

she saunters, she cycles but never regrets.

he ought to build dreams without any bricks,

and defend all honor without guns or sticks.

he ought to just be there for hugs and/or kicks

and deliver the moon dust, like a sorcerer does tricks.

she ought to rethink; yardstick and tape measure

the weight of the wait; the grail and the treasure

the love of the soul; the size of the pleasure

control by His grace; dream maker and sensor.

-end-

Not Knowing

I dated vigorously in the era in which women were liberated. As Victorian traditions unfolded into post-modern social chaos, love was free and pain was cheaper. I found much joy and was also dragged down long roads to nowhere, like a tin can tied to the bumper of a '57 Chevy. In the end, every moment was worth it.

Not Knowing

Easy come, easy go, and which one she'll be

nobody knows.

A lady here, a woman there, a child becoming all at once
and yet never the same.

Her beauty is an opiate, always promising and yet
delivering only more promises, mixed with promises of
searching,

furthermore,

for that certain balance in love, but where?

Is it a balance among moments of joy and despair;

tinkering pangs of satisfaction

and relentlessly insatiable pleas of flight –

that pleading flight that compels and enlarges,

that stretches and strengthens,

that elates and beleaguers the soul.

I wait; I wonder; I live; I love;

I will both give love and accept love;

and grow and find;

and yet,

never know . . .

what is . . .

that which is found!

-end-

Stuck or Lost

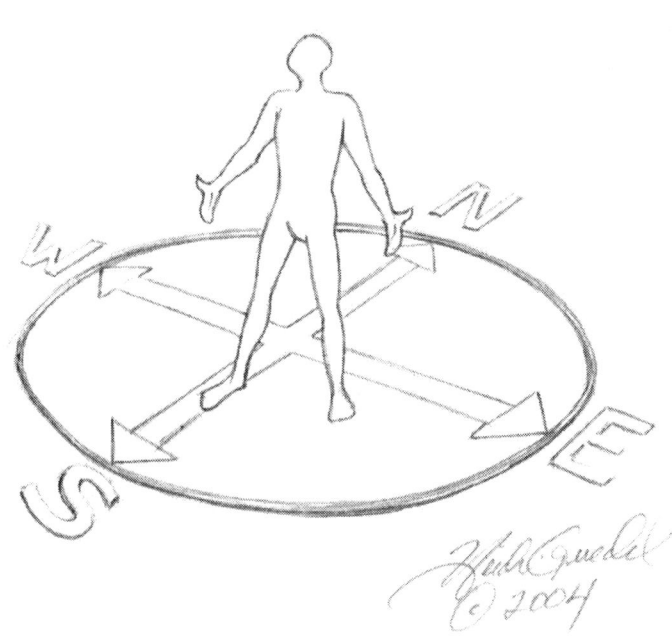

I hate songs about L.A. (pronounced - ehlle' lahy). People whining about the stuff they have and don't want or want and don't have. Meanwhile, they stay there and expect me to care.

These are my whining moments when I wanted to write and I couldn't. Or my imagination was transfixed by something vague. That vagueness was swirling in many tones and patterns of emotional and intellectual "stuff". My imagination, that vagueness, the patterns and tones . . . none of it would deliver any clarity. These are moments adjacent to perfection.

A Diminished Echo

So many thoughts in our lives come and go that we seldom pause to even consider the shear volume. Once, like awakening from a dream, I had a pleasant and rich thought that slipped away. As it did, I regretted the loss and savored the taste of the recent memory.

My mind then turned to the fragile nature of passing thoughts.

A Diminished Echo

a thought came to me
the other day
profoundly sweet like
mid-winter's rose.

I held it from
wind's ruthless sway.
while its scented drift
linked my mind,
like a beveled mirror,
to time.
a smile reflected and echoed
diminishing at each turn.

a droneful moment slept undisturbed.
a shadow was lightly etched.
slight recollections recant the day
but the thought has passed away.

-end-

UNMIND

When someone asks, "do you mind?" there is a subtle exchange of concerns. The questioner is "minding" something and is concerned about the other person's state of mind on that matter.

When I once exchanged poetry with a friend (sometime in the late 80's), there was a significant mismatch in the tone of our respective work. Her work was dark and heavy, potent and unsettling.

This was my reaction. I heard something vague and romantic in her work. But I couldn't see it until I tried it myself. It is the vivid imagery of TV violence presented in highly potent phrases.

I (personally) felt uneasy with my own familiarity with the details of such hollywood ho hum.

UNMIND

here, take this.

it's a dagger hewn of stainless words.

I'll guide your inquiring fingers around

its sculpted grip

to avoid a careless slip.

hold it as firmly as your intentions

and slide it deep between my ribs.

silently, bloodlessly, I'll let you go from there

to jab,

        or rip, or   scream,

        or stare

as my filament oozes, drips, burns,

or sags in moments reminisced,

like roses, shit, love and dishes

stacked, but not unmind.

-end-

I Saw Jesus Standing in the Grocery Store

This is dedicated to my friends Rex and Steve. Together, as my brothers on a long journey, they have instructed my soul in more ways than they can ever understand.

This is a tale of daily faith, lived with a vital energy and tuned to love. It's the everyday place that rings such a sweet tone.

I Saw Jesus at the Grocery Store

I saw Jesus in the grocery store the other day. He was standing next to Elvis in the produce department. They were both squeezing tomatoes and looking a little wistful, kinda like they were thinking about juicy homemade burgers that needed just the right tomato.

I knew right away it was Him. It was like looking up at an August high-noon sun. After just a second, my heart started to ache like a bee must feel when he can't flap another wing until he goes back to the hive to unload the nectar. When I recognized Him I felt compelled to stillness; so I could dwell safely in peace. And at the same time, I felt compelled to mad raving; so that everyone else could see Him, too.

No one else even noticed Him. As I stood there paralyzed, two people told me I was in their way. Then a woman stopped and said, "Don't you ever think about anyone else?" I stopped for a moment. Then I said, with only a tiny bit of desperation in my voice, "Yes, I do, I think of other people a lot. As a matter of fact, do you have two seconds to meet someone?"

She was an affluent, well-spoken woman. She said calmly and deliberately, "Not only are you inconsiderate, but you are pretentious, rude and your socks don't match." She marched off right towards Him and I thought surely she would see. But then she just reached right by Him, grabbed an avocado, twirled like a model on a runway and headed for the low-fat, anti-cholesterol high-fashion yogurt.

Just after she left, a small boy, maybe three years old, walked up to Him slowly and took a tiny fistful of His robe. They both just stood there, grinning. Soon, his big sister came over and tried to peel his little fingers away. As she did, she brushed His robe as well. The kids looked at each other. Then they both looked up at Him waited for a long moment. I carry bronzed tokens in my heart of those kids looking up at Him. They both hovered in the silence floating on His light. It was something like when you tilt your head just a little when you wait for the cuckoo clock to strike. It made them all happy.

Then the children walked away hand in hand. Somehow, they both looked taller.

I stood there for a long time studying His eyes and His movements. I wanted everyone to see Him, to meet Him, to know Him. And yet, He was clearly content to just be there amongst the people.

Some people abruptly avoided Him. Others looked for long moments, as if they recognized Him from their past. One guy even spoke to Him. He said, "Didn't we go to high school together?" The question was met with a grin as the man continued, "You moved away, didn't you? And Jesus replied, "No, I still live here." Then the guy left.

Lots of people came by. Nobody paid much attention. All I could do was stand there. When He walked out, He said to me, "A mature bee gathers lots of nectar, but he knows that to make honey he must bring it back to the hive."

Then I had to leave. Too many people were making a fuss over Elvis!

Matter of Mind

Interplay between words and ideas is a fascinating thing to study. We get things cute, like puns, and sophisticated like humor and double entendre.

This is an extended progression of words and ideas that flow together into an intricate complex of meanings that are both cute and compelling.

Matter of Mind

Mental fatigue means freedom
Yet mental freedom is fatiguing.
Bodily work means freedom
Yet bodily freedom requires work.
Justified love is not clear
And clearly love is not just.

Somewhere a man's mind can rest
And somewhere men rest and don't mind
for true mind cares not about matter
and the truth's just a matter of mind.

-end-

Surrounded

Thinking and observing are associated in ways that plunge deeply into cognitive science. Then again, the same association is the very basis of our everyday lives. While it is not necessary to add learning theory and cognition to our every thought, I suggest that we don't very often contemplate our surroundings as one contiguous 'thing'. In this poem, I do.

Surrounded

surroundings may whisper
or surroundings may pound
they have no intentions
except to surround.

enveloped by murmurs
or pierced by a shriek
they hasten by, intent on naught
so brief the existence they seek.

like despair in the cry of the baby,
or hope in the song of a bird,
nothing is blessed with permanence
like that of the written word.

it's born in the mind of the writer
and nourished by the hand and the pen,
implanted in a tomb of silence
resurrected one then maybe when.

it can lay in a scrawl
or an overpass wall
or induce reverence in one and all.

a curse or a lie
would never deny
what its author sought to imply.

con't

so once surrounded

by sounds

of surroundings now in sight,

an illusive dose of reality

consumes my earned respite.

I wonder at its image,

climb timidly towards its peak

as mysteries woven surround me

and my written words won't speak.

-end-

A Dog's Life

The idea behind this piece was born early in my writing career. I had noticed how people who hang out together really keep to themselves in a lot of ways – they "bark" about the same things.

The simplicity of a child's view seemed more appropriate than anything deep and complex. There is something absolute about the loneliness and despair of a life led inside of privately constructed fences.

A Dog's Life

There was a dog named Butch. He lived in our
backyard. He was big. I was sorry for him because he
never could get outside because the neighbors didn't
like him. He lived his whole life in our backyard. He
knew our backyard real good, all the bushes and the
fence, too. He always walked around the fence, but
he couldn't see through it. He never wanted to get out
except sometimes, when things happened outside.
Then he made lots of noise. When he was first growing
up he would jump real hard at the same time, then he
could see over a little. Then later, he didn't jump, but still
made lots of noise. Mom said it was because he didn't
understand. Dad said it was because he was stupid.
He was happy 'cause he had friends. He never knew
them because they had to stay in their backyards too.
He would make lots of noise when his friends did, even
when he couldn't see why they were making noise. I
think they just liked to make noise together. All other
times he would eat or sleep or play. After he got old, he
didn't make noise anymore. He would just walk around
the backyard and dig up old bones and bury them in a
different place. When his friends made noise, he would
try to sleep.

One day he got too old and died. We buried him and we
all cried, even some of the neighbors.

Sad Times

Sadness sets up a magnetic field between my pen and me. Whether it is noted by doodling or writing, slow pensive emotions move at a more approachable pace than does joy.

Stuck or Standing

I felt a strange sort of loneliness at times. They were strewn along arid and fruitless stretches in my life. As a rugby player, I was expected to behave certain ways, almost as a performance for those who would feed vicariously on my adventures.

Sometimes I would wonder about a life so filled with empty drama.

Stuck or Standing

rightfully written hopefully stricken, the mind meanders at will. I can't help but feel the painfully surmounted facts.

no place, no body, nothing.

somehow misplaced, personally disgraced without direction or balance - those facts blow from hither to yon.

beyond all the days and frivolous ways, there stands a place to be . . . to be without, or with (far less) that blur of memories cast.

rhythm undone.

the words don't flow, they linger and stick as the sharpest of feelings try to slide past. they won't.

they won't slide.

they won't pass.

here they remain motionless, unwilling to fade or blend.

they stand as a mountain once risen and now they only respect time.

they are jagged - those feelings - they know no form but their own and they stand through torrents of time.

time passes. they stand. they stand. time passes.

the facts stand like granite cliffs, lofting shadows onto themselves, then each other, as the day sets.

purity refuses to yield.

-end-

Trembling Within

Once, as I walked through an art gallery housed in an old mansion, I happened to pass under a spectacular chandelier. There were some high windows in the room but the sunlight could not be seen directly. It came from a side and blasted some storybook rays across the room and onto a wall with textured wallpaper and dark wooden trim. Those sunbeams were passing through the silence with refined indifference.

As I looked up, I was stung by the direct beacon of a solid ray of light that had made its way through the crystals hanging so orderly, so silently. And although it was instantaneous, it scorched my memory with an odd universal sense of perfection.

Trembling Within

a voice trembles within.

the words needed to relieve it are suspended

like the most regal chandelier.

each word of every sentence well defined

with fine crisp lines.

each one pure, each one hung silently

in the company of the others.

ordered and balanced, yet unique

and then without apparent discretion,

one perfectly directed ray of light

is refracted and penetrates the assembled mass

and exiting like a trumpeted blast, it purifies a soul.

that moment eclipsing, deposits one thought, one solitary spark.

but it has been so radiantly lit

that a heart is momentarily blinded,

drenched in light so complete,

that a tarnished mind can shine,

it's focused now on beauty that does exist

and awaits only to be seen.

can't

silently the thought is clarified.

now verbalized, the voice rises to speak.

sound won't stir the stillness.

the seconds count.

the feeling fades.

hope is exhaled back into the whole.

mind and heart harmoniously ache

at what was . . . and is no longer

the pen of the poet lends ear

to the silence of that light.

-end-

Awakening

This lyric fell upon me one day as I was driving through an old neighborhood in Dallas. I began to arrange two parallel, yet contradictory comments. As I saw that they could possibly be born as fraternal twins with contrary opinions, I could only pause to think.

Awakening

TRAPPED WITHIN I MUST GET OUT
THIS MIND-MADE COFFIN SEALED TIGHT WITH DOUBT

i noticed one cool and calm October eve the

LONG STEEL NAILS FORGED WELL WITH TIME
INSURING AGAINST A CREATIVE CRIME

inspiring air so clean and brisk

THAT MOTTLES THE MIND AND DISARRAYS THOUGHT
AND SAFELY CONFUSES THOSE THINGS UNTAUGHT

that direct my mind towards freedom unknown.

WHERE MENTAL MEANDERINGS, JUST SO ALIGNED
FORCIBLY FREE A SOUL REDEFINED

and allow me to write of things I feel.

re-Awakening

TRAPPED WITHIN I MUST GET OUT
THIS MIND-MADE COFFIN SEALED TIGHT WITH DOUBT

LONG STEEL NAILS FORGED WELL WITH TIME
INSURING AGAINST A CREATIVE CRIME

THAT MOTTLES THE MIND AND DISARRAYS THOUGHT
AND SAFELY CONFUSES THOSE THINGS UNTAUGHT

WHERE MENTAL MEANDERINGS, JUST SO ALIGNED
FORCIBLY FREE A SOUL REDEFINED

i noticed one cool and calm October eve the

inspiring air so clean and brisk

that directs my mind towards freedom unknown.

and allows me to write of things I feel.

-end-

Collisions of Wealth and Woe

In 1983, I had the dubious honor of dating a debutante. Over several weeks, I was exposed to a world of wealth that was foreign to me. There, amongst her friends, a tragedy was discussed in which one of "them", a thirty-year-old local boy, had been involved in more trouble than he could handle. Jack Daniels and cocaine were his bitter enemies posed as the sirens of Titan. It was all pretty amusing and met with light-hearted dismissiveness. Until, that is, the day he killed a kid with his car.

(He was returning from a charity function that night. He had been a smash hit among the dowagers that evening.)

This is my attempt to map his lostness.

Collisions of Wealth and Woe

"Stop trying to sense the world.

Your perceptual grasp is paralytic.

It's capacity is maimed by images of indulgence.

They swim in your mind and drip into your heart.

There they can decay even crystalline intent."

when first the words were said to me, i stood as a stone.

like the stone that is now in my heart.

momentous materials enriched my veins

so that the air never cleared from the dazzle.

activities, art, love and muscled mind

(realized, intensified and sensualized)

now fertilize my macho mirth.

its stench is of whisky, perfume and wet fur.

certainly growth was resultant.

but the weeds were sown with wheat.

so strengthened from wheat's modest nourishment,

atrophied with electronic bombardment.

weeded radioactivity, mad genuine artificial synthetics.

so false socio-plastic sterility has become the venom of
our doom

like the drink and the drugs that race through my veins.

while charities clamored, like a dove's flapping wings

like the drink and the drugs that shine in my veins

and the money amassed fueled the fire

like the drink and the drugs that inflate in my veins

and the carnal candies told hormonal lies

like the drink and drugs that carouse in my veins

con't

my jaguar slithered through streets in this town

like the drink and the drugs that collide in my veins

and of all the nightmarish fiascoes

(romantic, financial, among peers)

it's this torture that pounds my heart to stone.

i've just killed a kid with my car.

why do those words come back to me now.

"Stop trying to sense the world.

Your perceptual grasp is paralytic,

stressed by images of indulgence.

They swim in your mind and drip into your heart.

There they can decay even crystalline intent."

-end-

Confusion's Debris

At times my thinking cycles into something very much like a melody of ideas. I stand still in a universal setting in which the idea of 'now' is somehow inadequate. There is more to the moment than just 'now'. There is something clear and timeless about it.

One day, I found myself in anticipation of my two girls and my wife coming into the kitchen for breakfast. I thought about that anticipation for a while as I finished getting everything ready.

Later that day, I reflected thoroughly on that anticipation.

Confusion's Debris

standing knee deep in confusion's debris,
I doubt most things in view.

a silent shroud of disharmony lingers in the air
like an aroma,
it hangs heavy like a bowl full of raw eggs
whipped and ready to be scrambled
for Sunday brunch.

then I blink.

like a passing L-train, the roar of disquiet rumbles away
and leaves a new clarity in the stillness.
the weight of things passing
lifts the awareness of the gifts that are hidden in my day,
gifts that are present always, like the cracks in the
sidewalk
and the dusty trail of broken leaves and twigs and dirt
tracked in on moving sneakers and clogs and flip-flops,
the trail that links my home to everything else that is
outside.

every leafy crumb on my carpet is evidence of lighter
things that also pass,
my children and their friends,
my wife and her endless motion,

(con't)

my old just-let-me-sleep cat, annoyed by my teen kitten,

remnants of chores and things that are yet undone

all float in

stay for several whiles

and pass by

leaving little vapor trails of whimsy and woe

mixed in with things destined for a vacuum cleaner bag . . .

someday.

because to my life,

it is the clutter of what is left behind

that builds up

like that salty metallic crud around a faucet.

(the water moves so fast, how does that stuff get there?)

it's just like confusion's debris . . .

rarely is it all gone,

even rarer are times that it is not accumulating in stealth
mode.

but when the brink comes and the world

. . . which usually holds its shape like an eggshell . . .

cracks under pressure,

you scrape away the crud with deliberate squinting
postures . . .

you finish whipping the scrambled clingy yellowness

now submitting to be your hope served up in a breakfast
taco.

I take a deep breath and wait for the door to open,

for the room to fill with hunger that can be quenched with
what has become fluffy.

(con't)

I wait for some meaningless thing to fill the air with the music of laughter,

the knowing smiles of my wife,

and beneath that which has been scraped away

there is new hope in the stillness

tracked into my life

from outside . . .

outside both my view and my understanding.

and when the air stirs and life is scented by tales of the day

my world shuffles and tilts

in rhythm

with the telling

and things pass away

leaving new aromas in the air.

so it's only when I stand around,

that I get knee deep in confusion's debris.

so I'd rather not.

excuse me, I've got to go.

Late one night sitting on the edge of coordinated trends in life and love, in business and career. (Oct 2001)

Pitter Patter

I have written poetry in many settings and many states of mind. One state is the only slightly slurred thinking at a certain level of drunkenness. It isn't completely nonsense and yet it isn't completely coherent.

The day I wrote this, I was alone in the house and it was raining. I don't remember the circumstances, but I remember the aching notion that I didn't want to be there alone.

Pitter Patter

pitter patter, pitter patter
ping pang, ping pang pong

glitter clatter, glitter clatter
whiz bang, bing bang bong

when up on the roof there arose such a clatter
that I sprang from my bed to quiet the chatter

my head so too full
my soul too empty

I fled from the dread
I bled good-and-plenty

images homages, think thank thunk
pizzing and pazzing, drink drank drunk

I hate all beer, except the one that draws near
I resent the booze, except the one that I choose
I loathe the desire, 'cept the pleasin' fire
I can't wait to quit, but this one's lit
I think on the past, but it don't last
I find someone new, but she's worthless too,
I ache and I burn, but I can't seem to learn,

(con't)

She's immortal and strong, but sweet in the song.

I hate what I love, if its not from above

But I listen and wait, my own Watergate

It stinks and it stunk, I hate when I'm drunk

my mind burns my eyes and I see only lies

it won't go away, but it rots as I stay

so I step on the stage and can't find a sage

to teach and to preach, to lean and to reach

the frat boy inside, the paternalized side

I hate what I am, in a fractalized sham

but tomorrow I'll stop . . .

if not . . .

I will pound on my brain and stop the refrain,

pitter patter, pitter patter

bing bang bong

I hate being alone, when it rains.

I'm drunk.

-end-

Pneumatics

Sometimes I am driven to write things down. So many of my thoughts are comprehensively illusive, I quiver when one ripens and takes shape. Then for a little while, I live in a suspended reality. The scene starts telling me secrets and reflections bounce around like a rainy night on Times Square. I drink the images up like happy hour cold ones and before I notice, I am in the stupor of a geometric progression of peace.

The Seed Released

This is my personal favorite. I don't remember writing it. I know that is was during a long murky time in my life when career was colliding with rugby frolic and feminine frenzy was competing with deep seeded needs for a true committed relationship. I felt lost and lonely when alone and I was too busy playing most of the time to care.

Amidst all this, I wrote The Seed Released.
I found it in my desk many months later.

The Seed Released

the seed released drifts freely
to become friend or victim of powers that be
it rolls and tumbles or hides
in an earth well-textured with time . . .
then it rests, unplanted
and waits, not knowing what sleeps within.

until circumstantial blessings surround it
and water and air, earth and sun conspire
and growth somehow begins
a new life has not been created, only permitted.

enlightened and nourished by an ever-giving sun
cooled and refreshed by water passing by
formed and caressed by still air and storm
and attached to one place on the earth.

uprooted and changed adapted then bent
hopes well directed, with energies spent
the time and each goal, once arrived, went.

and an aching man with an empty heart
digs for his roots, someplace to start
and the only clue left, is the 'missing' part

not the pieces foreseen weaving the whole
or the stories recorded by the collective soul
but that moment, which fate, from his memory stole

con't

that moment held peace, simple and clear
it guarded his hopes and kept away tears
and carefully mindfully whispered, "God nears."

no longer young, still not yet old
youth's confidence withers but tries to be bold
and aspiring dreams are retired untold.

And unfilled dreams, like limbs freshly pruned, lie green
for a while unknowing. They lay unaffected. They don't
gasp for air or struggle towards water. They rot or burn
with indifference. They have a place in death as they did
in life. And in dying, it can't be forgotten that they had
life, they gave shade and rustled in the wind.

And the seeds they released, drifted freely.

-end-

Mosaics

While some of my pieces begin with the turn of a phrase, others are born with an image. Mosaics was long in gestation. I had the image of my mind being composed of colorful little pebbles –each distinct in shape, size and color. I dwelt on that mental picture for a long time.

Then one day this poured out, I never intended nor designed any rhyming pattern. It came out in the spill.

mosaics

hidden among the pebbles

of the mosaic in my mind

sleeps sincere significance

not manufactured and not designed.

like water on its downward flow

can never be misaligned

and sentiment when deeply felt

will no further be refined.

so I eagerly go on journeys

of both spectacular and common kind

to discover transparent blessings

in souls eco-socially maligned

by discolored harmonic patterns

contracted, confirmed but unsigned,

as societal heroic absurdity

becomes lust and poor judgment enshrined.

yet they build still a pleasant picture

such a spectrum of hopes so entwined

the visions are brilliant and simple

like wisps of sea spray to the blind.

they whisper secrets, each a hue of the truth,

depositing crystals behind

sprouting kaleidoscopic memories,

a mosaic one stone at a time.

-end-

OKAY

All forms of art have touched me profoundly at different times in my life. The Broadway play Equus was one such production. It was pungent emotionally and powerful, graceful and disturbing all at the same time. I got to see it twice, once with Anthony Perkins in the lead, the second time Richard Burton played the same role. In one of the scenes, the character – an off balance psychiatrist trying to help a young boy – turns to the audience and wonders how events are captured in the mind of a child. What set of circumstances trigger something in our brains that flick the switch and form a solid clear memory?

Here, I take this notion to a hopeful conclusion.

OKAY

the art of the artist moaned and wailed
and the prisoner repented for which he was jailed
a train of thought was lost and derailed
while billowing canvass, across the sea sailed.

they all shared the moment, the motion, the thought
and each by some memory was silently caught
as all thoughts began and passed on to naught
no meaning or curse was deliberately sought

yet still some significance prepared the way,
like the hands of the sculpture nurtures the clay
and a soul opens slowly by His efforts each day
so in a moment, uncluttered, one can see, "We're OK."

-end-

Coexistence

Harmonies in nature are everywhere. Although as humans we like to think we can actually alter global conditions, I personally don't buy it. Humanity is a component of the earth, just like our geological landscape or our atmosphere. You can argue about how (exactly) we got here or how the earth got here.

What you can't argue is that we are here together.

Coexistence

the land rises and curves,

is rocked and must yield

and the radiant core gives up

both the cliff and the field.

it brings forth its power

with the quakes and smelted ore

or awes us with stillness -

magnitude's subtle shore,

where magnitudes of man

must meet magnitudes of earth.

so we coexist in mysteries,

which permitted respective birth.

-end-

Silence

It was a quiet day in the park and all were enjoying the relative silence. Yes, there were birds twittering and wind blowing. Kids played off in the distance. But what caught my eye like a shooting star, was the interchange between an older woman, who had been sitting alone and a young mother meandering by with her baby in a stroller. In the stillness of that day, they volleyed with eye contact and saluted the relentless power of all children to renew the face of the earth. They cheered together, but never disrupted the silence we all shared. I was blessed to see it all and even more blessed to capture it in rhyme.

I only rarely find such complete joy. When the words came tumbling out, I had no direction in mind and certainly no cadence. Nor did I know where it would lead. I sat in a trance for about an hour as best I could remember.

I remember how blessed I felt to be able to see such beauty in an emotional exchange that universally captures the core relationships of humanity . . . the mother, the child and one that knows the bond. It's like candle lit-faces with singing hearts.

Silence

silence fertilizes my thoughts as they grow

from consciousness ignited from fuel I don't know.

some glow like burning embers,

other's fire works through the night.

some distort in turbulence,

what began in calm delight.

a rumbling, churning, grinding wheel

laughingly mocks the ideas it can steal.

when it dowses a spark

with noise or neglect

and dampens the warmth,

then negates the effect.

but times also come, when seeds can be planted

with day dreams or visions that must be enchanted,

when I see the spark in an old woman's eye,

when the baby and mother (unknown) just stroll by

reminiscent of childhood's laughter and tear

while diminishing aged societal fear

and the moment expands to consume everyone,

to envelop the dismal, elated, then some.

creating the fuel

that, surely, we need

GOD's love for the spark

and I'll spread the seed.

-end-

(There is no)

END

ABOUT THE AUTHOR

Born in Texas, raised in California, and college years on the East Coast, Derly Andre has heartfully captured the essence of suburban life in refined emotional detail. In reserved times, he traveled with "Up With People", where young people carried a wave of optimism to an aching population in the 1970s and, as a rugby player, he rode the crest of the singles life that echoed out of the sixties. He was a combatant in the sexual revolution and a watch-guard dad to two girls through the 90s. From hell-raiser to Sunday school teacher, from confirmed bachelor to dedicated family man, he always watched the cultural ebb and flow around him.

Through it all he was writing poetry. Derly's poetry was not written or compiled with this book in mind. It was always deeply personal – a scrapbook in word pictures. Pneumatrix is a tale of a pensive soul on a journey through the past 30 years. He is well known as a speaker on spiritual topics and still known in high tech circles as a visionary in his chosen field of information technology for medical informatics. He annoys his family with bad habits and occasionally takes 12 items through the 10-item express line. He has been functionally unemployed for almost three years and has been operating incognito as Chef Andre, ace pitchman for vegetable choppers. His deep commitment to his church family is his source of strength and comfort. He loves his life.

He writes for many lost young people and more who have made it through to the other side where memories and meanings are woven into tapestries that are uniquely colored and textured with common threads of our culture. As a student of human nature, he has graduated to this.

ABOUT THE ILLUSTRATOR

-Heidi Guedel is a professional artist with over 25 years experience in the feature animated film industry. Her many years of studio animation work were done in Glendale and Hollywood, California, where she earned screen credits working for Walt Disney Productions, Don Bluth Productions, and Warner Brothers Feature Animation. Her multiple screen credits earned her a membership in The Academy of Motion Picture Arts and Sciences in 1983, where she is proud to participate in voting for the Academy Awards (the "Oscars").

Heidi is one of the first women in animation since WWII to have been promoted to "animator" at Walt Disney Productions, and she is a published author. Her autobiography: Animatrix--A Female Animator, How Laughter Saved My Life - is garnering 5-STAR book reviews on Amazon.com. This professional history makes her signature all the more significant to collectors..

ABOUT THE PUBLISHER

TICO PUBLISHING is a small independent publisher specializing in unknown or first-time authors. We respect an artists' vision and work with authors to make their dreams of being published come true. We are not a vanity press. We review material for marketability and content and will finance, publish, market and distribute first-class quality books though major retailers like Amazon.com, and Barnes & Noble. We'll also get your vision copyrighted and on file with the Library of Congress and have an ISBN issued. We set up hardcover, soft cover and e-books for you as well as schedule and facilitate book signings and other promotional events.

If you like the quality of this book and have always dreamed of becoming a PUBLISHED author or have a finished work and are tired of getting rejection slips, contact us for more information on how we can assist you.

We welcome comments and suggestions as well as inquiries and manuscripts via e-mail for review at tijerin@yahoo.com

Our contact information is as follows:

TICO Publishing
25045 Jaclyn Avenue
Moreno Valley, CA 92557
(951) 452-2277

ORDER FORM

TICO Publishing
25045 Jaclyn Avenue
Moreno Valley, CA 92557

CHECK YOUR LEADING BOOKSTORE OR ORDER HERE

___ YES, I want ___ copies of *PNEUMATRIX: A POETIC SOUL* at $26.95 each, plus $4 shipping for the first book and $2 for each additional book. Canadian orders must be accompanied by a postal money order in U.S. funds. Allow 2-3 weeks maximum for delivery unless noted otherwise.

My check or money order for $_____ is enclosed.

Credit card orders can be placed through the Paypal online payment system by going to www.paypal.com and sending payment to tijerin@yahoo.com. Please specify the quantity and item you are ordering. You can also visit us online at www.apoeticsoul.com

Name_____

Organization_____

Address_____

City/State/Zip_____

Phone_____

Email _____

Please make your check payable to:

TICO Publishing
25045 Jaclyn Avenue
Moreno Valley, CA 92557
(951) 452-2277

Email: customerservice@apoeticsoul.com